CLASSICAL THEMES FOR TWO

Arrangements by Peter Deneff

ISBN 978-1-5400-1416-0

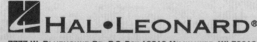

HAL•LEONARD®

7777 W. BLUEMOUND RD. P.O. BOX 13819 MILWAUKEE, WI 53213

In Australia Contact:
Hal Leonard Australia Pty. Ltd.
4 Lentara Court
Cheltenham, Victoria, 3192 Australia
Email: ausadmin@halleonard.com.au

ACADEMIC FESTIVAL OVERTURE

VIOLINS

By JOHANNES BRAHMS

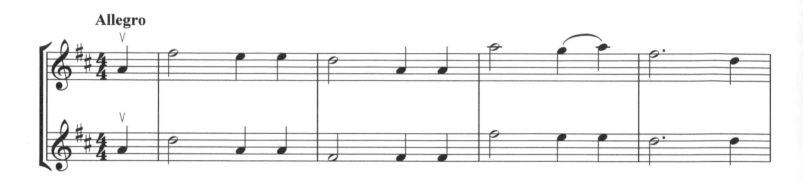

Slowly

AIR
from WATER MUSIC

VIOLINS

By GEORGE FRIDERIC HANDEL

Andante con moto

(small notes optional)

To Coda

AIR ON THE G STRING
from ORCHESTRAL SUITE NO. 3 IN D MAJOR, BWV 1068

VIOLINS

By JOHANN SEBASTIAN BACH

BLUE DANUBE WALTZ

VIOLINS

By JOHANN STRAUSS, JR.

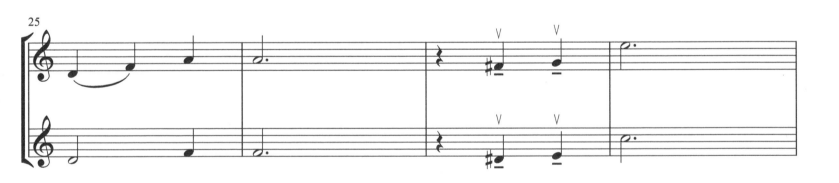

CANON IN D

VIOLINS

By JOHANN PACHELBEL

CLAIR DE LUNE
from SUITE BERGAMASQUE

VIOLINS

By CLAUDE DEBUSSY

EINE KLEINE NACHTMUSIK
(Second Movement Theme: "Romance")

VIOLINS

By WOLFGANG AMADEUS MOZART

FLOWER DUET

from LAKMÉ

VIOLINS

By LÉO DELIBES

HALLELUJAH CHORUS
from MESSIAH

VIOLINS

By GEORGE FRIDERIC HANDEL

(small note optional)

HORNPIPE
from WATER MUSIC

VIOLINS

By GEORGE FRIDERIC HANDEL

Allegro maestoso

HUNGARIAN DANCE NO. 5

VIOLINS

By JOHANNES BRAHMS

JESU, JOY OF MAN'S DESIRING
from CANTATA 147

VIOLINS

By JOHANN SEBASTIAN BACH

MARCH
from THE NUTCRACKER

VIOLINS

By PYOTR IL'YICH TCHAIKOVSKY

MINUET IN G
from ANNA MAGDALENA NOTEBOOK

VIOLINS

By CHRISTIAN PETZOLD
formerly attributed to J.S. Bach

ODE TO JOY
from SYMPHONY NO. 9 IN D MINOR

VIOLINS

By LUDWIG VAN BEETHOVEN

MORNING
from PEER GYNT

VIOLINS

By EDVARD GRIEG

Allegretto pastorale

PICTURES AT AN EXHIBITION
(Promenade)

VIOLINS

By MODEST MUSSORGSKY

POMP AND CIRCUMSTANCE
March No. 1

VIOLINS

By EDWARD ELGAR

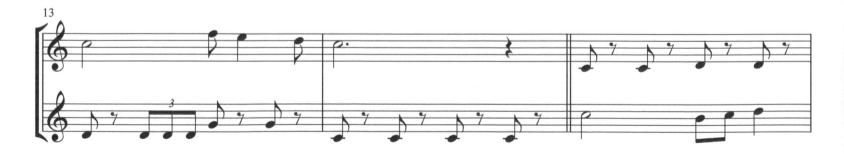

RONDEAU
from SUITE DE SYMPHONIE

By JEAN-JOSEPH MOURET

VIOLINS

SHEEP MAY SAFELY GRAZE
from CANTATA 208

VIOLINS

By JOHANN SEBASTIAN BACH

THE SURPRISE SYMPHONY
(Symphony No. 94, Second Movement Theme)

VIOLINS

By FRANZ JOSEPH HAYDN

SYMPHONY NO. 7
(Second Movement Theme)

VIOLINS

By LUDWIG VAN BEETHOVEN

TRUMPET VOLUNTARY
(Prince of Denmark's March)

VIOLINS

By JEREMIAH CLARKE

WILLIAM TELL OVERTURE
(Theme)

VIOLINS

By GIOACHINO ROSSINI